WOMEN
Pursuing
GOD

With

Perseverance

Persistence

Purpose

31-Day Journey

Frizella Taylor

Unless otherwise indicated, all scripture references are from
New International Version (NIV)
The Passion Translation (TPT)
New King James Version (NKJV)
Amplified Bible (AMP)

Women Pursuing GOD
With Perseverance Persistence Purpose
31-Day Journey

© November 2021
ISBN# 978-1-953526-22-9

All rights reserved under international copyright law. This book or parts thereof may not be reproduced in any form, stored in a retrieval system, or transmitted in any form by any means; electronic, mechanical, photocopy, recording, or otherwise without prior written permission of the publisher or author, except as provided by United States of America copyright.

Published by TaylorMade Publishing
Jacksonville, FL 32218
www.TaylorMadePublishingFL.com
(904) 323-1334

TaylorMade Publishing

Table of Contents

Introduction i

Day 1 - Persistent 1

Day 2 - Prayerful 4

Day 3 - Pliable 7

Day 4 - Prompt 10

Day 5 - Purpose 13

Day 6 - Persuasive 16

Day 8 - Provisions 22

Day 9 - Potential 25

Day 11 - Perpetuate 31

Day 12 - Proceed 34

Day 13 - Pursue 37

Day 14 - Press 40

Day 15 - Pain 43

Day 16 - Pertinacious 46

Day 17 - Pressure 49

Day 18 - Preserve 52

Day 19 - Protection 55

Day 20 - Process 58

Day 21 - Praise 61

Day 22 - Patience 64

Day 24 - Possibility 70

Day 25 - Passion 73

Day 26 - Pride 76

Day 27 - Pant 79

Day 28 - People 82

Day 29 - Promote 85

Day 30 - Plans 88

Day 31 - Promise 91

About the Author 95

Introduction

It's 2021, the year after the pandemic called coronavirus AKA COVID-19 practically shut down the world. Many people anxiously waited for 2020 to be over, anticipating that 2021 would come through with a greater hope for our society. However, the pandemic is still here, most are still required to wear masks, and many areas have experienced an uprising in COVID-19 cases.

Though we were careful, COVID-19 crept into our home. My husband was sick for 21 days and we had to quarantine in the house. I stayed in the guest room and used the front of the house, while he stayed in the master bedroom. During this time, the Lord spoke to me a word for this year. That word is "perseverance." I recall saying in response, "OK Lord, I hear you." But at the same time, I was not quite clear about his underlying thought for this word. Therefore, I waited for the Lord to bring clarification and intent to the message He was speaking to me.

One month later, February 1st, 2021, he unveiled directions to me. He said, "Daughter, write a 31-day consecration devotional to walk My people through the journey of pursuing Me and My will."

The dictionary defines **perseverance** as steady, persistence in a course of action, or a state, etc. especially in difficulties, obstacles, or discouragement. In theology, **perseverance** means continuing in a state of grace to the end, leading to eternal salvation. **Persistence** is to continue steadfastly or firmly in some state or purpose or course of action. **Purpose** is the reason in which something exists or is done. These three words in totality define how we will pursue God in this 31-day journey. We want to be so connected with Him that we become unmovable from Him, regardless of what happens in this world.

How fascinating! So, what does that mean for us in the next 31 days? We will walk through this journey consecrating ourselves to the Lord **"Pursuing God with Perseverance, Persistence and Purpose."** This 31-Day Journey will assist us in our personal pursuit to persevere towards the will of God for our lives. Enjoy the journey through each **"Pet P"** word of the day.

"Praying always with all prayer and supplication in the spirit, being watchful to this end with all perseverance and supplication for all the Saints."

Ephesians 6:18

Day 1 - Persistent

Today's word is persistent, it means lasting or enduring tenaciously.

When trials and tribulations come our way, the natural instinct is to succumb to the pressure. Some reach out to friends and family for advice or a listening ear. Some go into a state of depression and anxiety.

However, as we will see, there are some things God instructs us to do. Luke 11:9-10 (NIV) says, "So I say to you: Ask and it will be given to you; seek and you will find; knock and the door will be opened to you. For everyone who asks receives; the one who seeks finds; and to the one who knocks, the door will be opened."

We are to "ask, seek, and knock." These actions point us to continually approach God. What have you been seeking from the Lord? According to these scriptures, when we ask the Lord for something, He will give it to us. In other words, we will receive what we ask for.

"Ask" means to make a request; to inquire, or to put a demand on. "Seek" means trying to find or discover by searching or questioning. Then, there is the "knock," with the indication of banging on a door to be admitted in or as to calling attention to. The persistent knocking on the Lord's heart will definitely gain his attention.

We are encouraged in this scripture to "seek," to look for, and when we do, "it" will be found. We always hear people say desperate times call for desperate measures. So, we should continue to "ask, seek, and knock" until the door is opened, and we get favor allowing us to obtain the thing we are seeking.

Let's Pray:

Father, I come to You "asking, seeking, and knocking" for Your will for my life. I pray through and beyond every trial and tribulation to get into Your presence and to receive everything You have for me. I am ready to be persistent in searching for Your will and presence. In Jesus' name. Amen.

Thought for Today

Day 2 - Prayerful

Today's word is prayerful; it simply means given to, characterized by, or expressive of prayer; devout.

2 Chronicles 7:14 (NIV) says, "If my people, who are called by my name, will humble themselves and pray and seek my face and turn from their wicked ways, then I will hear from heaven, and I will forgive their sin and will heal their land."

In this day and time, we cannot allow our prayers to cease. We are encouraged in this verse to pray. However, there is so much more in this scripture the Lord wants us to know. Before we get to this verse, we should understand that King Solomon made a sacrifice before the Lord and dedicated the temple to God. Think about how we would do this today.

This scripture also mentioned that we should humble ourselves; pray and seek the Lord. Humbling ourselves can be a tough thing to do when we are so used to doing everything ourselves and our way. To be humble is simply to submit to the power and the will of God, posturing ourselves in a position of inferiority to Him. We do this in order to hear, receive, and pray according to His will and not our own selfish desires.

"Seek" in this verse is to crave or long for the presence and will of the Lord as a necessity. "Wicked ways" here refers to their lack of prayer. When we seek the Lord, we begin to crave Him, spend time with Him and hear from Him. He becomes our necessity, our "I've got to have Him." That is when the Lord will hear us; he will forgive our sin and restore us. So, why not be healed and restored?

Let's Pray:

Father, I come to You asking for an increase in my prayer life. I humble myself before You and call on You as I seek your face. I ask that You search my heart for anything that is not like You. Forgive me of anything I may have said or done so that my prayers will be answered. In Jesus' name. Amen.

Thought for Today

Day 3 - Pliable

Today's word is pliable, which means easily bent; flexible; supple; adaptable or adjusting readily to change.

You may be asking why you would want to be pliable. I'm so glad you asked. When it comes to pursuing the will of God for our lives, we want to be pliable. To be pliable in the Lord's hands simply means we are willing to exchange our plans for His plans. It is being bendable in our lifestyle, personal ways, family traditions, and more.

When we say yes to the Lord, He will take us out of our comfort zone. The prophet Isaiah says this in chapter 6:8, "Then I heard the voice of the Lord saying, whom shall I send? And who will go for us? And I (Isaiah) said, "Here am I. Send me!"

Can we be like Isaiah and say, 'Here am I send me?' He did so without knowing the details of what he was getting into. Because later, Isaiah asks the Lord in verse eleven, "For how long Lord?" When the Lord sends you, He will let you know when that time is up.

In addition, we can take the stance that Mary took when she was visited by the angel who informed her that she was chosen to birth Jesus into the world. Luke 1:38 (NIV) says, "I am the Lord's servant," Mary answered. "May your word to me be fulfilled." Then the Angel left her." Are you the Lord's servant? Are you ready to fulfill the word and assignment given to you? Then you must become pliable in the Lord's hand.

Let's Pray:

Father, I commit myself to You from this moment forward; I submit to being pliable in Your hands. I am Your servant, and I am ready to fulfill the assignment You have given me. I decrease that You may increase in my life, Holy Spirit have Your way with me. In Jesus, name. Amen.

Thought for Today

Day 4 - Prompt

Today's word is prompt, which means done, performed, delivered; without delay; ready in action.

Sometimes we hear the voice of the Lord and doubt it; we try to figure it out or simply don't discern it as the Lord's voice. However, in the instances where we know it is the Lord's voice, how quick are we to respond?

It's important to not only respond quickly but to know how to respond. But in order to respond, we first have to believe. Jesus spoke to Thomas in John 20:29 (NIV) saying, "Because you have seen me, you have believed; blessed are those who have not seen and yet have believed."

This serves as a reminder that when we hear the Lord, we do not have to ask for a sign that it is Him; we should believe. The more time we spend with the Lord, the better we are at recognizing His voice when He speaks to us.

The other side of "prompt" is when the Holy Spirit prompts us to do something for someone else. This also requires a response from us. Our response here is to listen for complete orders and directions for the assignment that He has given. This is not a time for us to doubt the Lord's voice, but a time to acknowledge it for the assignment He is speaking to us.

Let's Pray:

Father God, I thank You for speaking to me. I ask that I fine-tune my spiritual ears to hear You clearer and be ready to move timely in the direction You speak to me. Lord, help me to hear You. In Jesus, name. Amen.

Thought for Today

Day 5 - Purpose

Today's word is *purpose*, which means the reason for which something exists or is done, made, used, etc. It also means an intended or desired result; end; aim; goal.

Each of us has a purpose for being here. Some of us know what the purpose is, and some of us may not. Some know bits and pieces of their purpose, but not enough to feel they can move forward in that purpose.

The apostle Paul taught in Romans 8:28 (TPT), "So we are convinced that every detail of our lives is continually woven together for good, for we are his lovers who have been called to fulfill his designed purpose."

Each part of our lives is and will be used by the Lord to fulfill the call He has for us individually and some collectively. So, how do we find our God-given purpose? First and foremost, the general will of God is found in His Word, the Bible. Then, we can start with the list of things we are passionate about. This is not always the things we know how to do. The Lord will prepare us for our passion, even if it means we must go to school, do some specialized training, or even if we have to sit under the leadership of someone currently doing what we are passionate about.

Our job is to pray, to seek the Lord and allow Him to speak to us and show us our purpose. In addition, we can volunteer in several ways in the local church and charities to see if the Lord speaks to our heart about any of those activities. We aren't to just sit idly until the Lord speaks. Ecclesiastes 9:10a (NIV) says this, "Whatever your hand finds to do, do it with all your might."

Prayer

Father, I come before Your presence seeking Your purpose for my life. I lay down my ways and offer myself to You that I may be used for Your glory. Reveal my purpose to me. In Jesus' name. Amen.

Thought for Today

Day 6 - Persuasive

Today's word is persuasive, meaning to have the ability to persuade. To persuade is to induce to believe by appealing to reason or understanding; it is to convince.

Our society makes it a little difficult to persuade others to follow Christ. It makes one take a good look at how others see us. Are we looking like Christ? Do our actions or responses reflect our belief in Christ?

I have learned the first evangelistic tool is my actions. My mom used to say to us, "You represent me when you are outside." That is how we should be in our daily lives as we display Christ, we represent Him.

Therefore, we should be ready to speak of our faith at any moment. We are reminded by apostle Paul in 2 Corinthians 5:11 (TPT), "Since we are those who stand in holy awe of the Lord, we make it our passion to persuade others to turn to him. We know that our lives are transparent before the God who knows us fully, and I hope that we are also well known to your consciences."

To walk out this scripture, we must be constantly in His (the Lord's) face, listening to his leading, prompting, and instructions. This leading will assist us in living a persuasive lifestyle. Living a life of transparency is not always easy, however, the Bible tells us in Revelation 12:11a (NIV), "They triumphed over him by the blood of the Lamb and by the word of their testimony." So, sometimes we have to share parts of our lives when we minister to others, which causes them to be persuaded.

Let's Pray:

Father, I pray for a persuasive heart, that I will be willing to share Your grace and mercy to those whom I come across when You speak to me about them. Make me a living sacrifice, knowing that my testimony will bring about change in someone's life. In Jesus' name. Amen.

Thought for Today

Day 7 - Polite

Today's word is polite, which means to show good manners towards others, as in behavior.

I often think about how people feel when someone attempts to share the gospel of Jesus Christ with them. I have observed over the years how rude some Christians can be when approaching the assumed non-believer.

There is a time and place for everything. The truth being told, when we want to share anything with others, we should take the opportunity to display a spirit of politeness. That is being thoughtful, patient, kind, courteous, and grateful. Why should we do this?

Because the word of God teaches us in Colossians 4:2-6, "Devote yourself to prayer, being watchful and thankful. And pray for us, too, that God may open a door for our message, so that we may proclaim the mystery of Christ, for which I am in chains. Pray then I may proclaim it clearly, as I should. Be wise in the way you act towards outsiders. make the most of every opportunity. Let your conversation be always full of grace, seasoned with salt, so that you may know how to answer everyone."

When we are in God's presence with prayer, praise, and thanksgiving, it changes our hearts, the way we speak to others, that is, our conversation. We can pray this same prayer for ourselves that we too, proclaim the gospel with clarity and wisdom.

Let's Pray:

Father I pray Colossians 4:2-6 over my life, that I am devoted to prayer, and I am watchful and thankful. I pray for opportunities to share Your message. I ask for wisdom on what that looks like, and I pray that my conversation is seasoned with grace and salt as I minister to others. In Jesus' name. Amen.

Thought for Today

Day 8 - Provisions

Today's word is provisions, which means the providing or supplying of something; the meeting of needs; the supplying of means.

There is no one who can say they do not need, require, or desire provisions. We cannot put our total trust in the job we have, the business we own, or our spouse or parents.

Each of those are tools or means the Father uses to provide for us. We cannot trust the systems of the world to be the sole supplier of what we need. We know it is not our talents or our abilities that bring us total provisions.

How do we know that? Because many people with higher degrees do not make the money they thought they would when they decided upon the degree choice. Many people have to settle for lesser paying positions to provide for their families. Then there are some people who cannot understand how their needs are met because they have a minimum wage job and a high yield faith life.

Paul teaches us in Philippians 4:19 (NIV), "And my God will meet all your needs according to the riches of his glory in Christ Jesus."

So, regardless of our careers or lack thereof, our faith in the word of God and the wisdom of God, plus our trust in the Lord and the leading of Holy Spirit, significantly increases our provisions . Keep in mind our current position is a tool in God's hand.

Let's Pray:

Father, I thank You for supplying my need. I understand You use my career as a tool, and for that I am thankful; I pray for the continual supply from You as I link my faith to Your word. Thank You for being a God of abundance. In Jesus' name. Amen.

Thought for Today

Day 9 - Potential

Today's word is potential, which means possible, as opposed to actual; it is capable of being or becoming.

Each of us has potential locked up within us. You and I have the potential to be successful in our careers, in our marriages, with child rearing, and in our God-given ministry or calling.

However, it will take us exercising our faith to believe and receive from God, what He said we can do, and who we are in Him. We have the potential for greatness. Potential can be converted to actual. Paul the apostle said in Philippians 4:13 (NIV), "I can do all this through him who gives me strength (power or encouragement)." What has the Lord asked you to do? Why are you afraid of stepping out?

When we know what we're supposed to do, then, we prepare ourselves in the natural the best way possible. In doing so, be submitted to the Lord's leading by His Holy Spirit. Give that talent to the Lord as a service. You will find that locked up potential will become a reality and it will actually happen. So, why not unleash your potential by unleashing your faith?

Lastly, remember, faith without works is dead. We can have all the faith in the world and believe God for the impossible. But if we never step out on what He is asking us to do, then that bottled up potential never becomes a reality. So, let's go!

Let's Pray:

Father I come to You asking for directions and leading of the plans and purposes for my life. I ask for the release of potential within me and that I understand what You are speaking to me. Lord, please grace me with the ability to act on what You are doing in my life. In Jesus' name. Amen.

Thought for Today

Day 10 - Pleasure

Today's word is pleasure, which means the state of being pleased; it is a source of enjoyment or delight.

For the most part, when we think of pleasure, our mind tends to go in the direction of fleshy gratification or satisfaction. We all know the world's view of pleasure leads us away from the presence of the Lord. It teaches all about self-love while the Bible teaches us to love our neighbors as ourselves (Mark 12:31).

So, we should adjust our focus of "Pleasure" to see it through the lens of God. What we have learned as pleasure is not pleasure at all. Psalms 147:11 (NIV) tells us, "The Lord delights in those who fear him, who put their hope in his unfailing love."

Did you know that you can take pleasure in the Lord? Let's look at Psalms 37:4-5 (TPT). It says, "Find your delight and true pleasure in Yahweh, and he will give you what you desire the most. Give God the right to direct your life, and as you trust him along the way, you'll find he pulled it off perfectly!"

When we take pleasure in the Lord, it opens the opportunity for Him to do supernatural things for us as well as giving us the desires of our hearts. What do you desire? Are you willing to take pleasure in the Lord as a lifestyle? Are you willing to delight yourself in the Lord and put your hope in Him?

Let's Pray:

Father, I thank you for the opportunity to dwell in your presence and delight in You. I ask You to show me the true way of pleasure in and through You. I submit to You whole-heartedly as my Lord and Savior. I trust You to lead me in the direction I should go, and I pray that I will not allow the world's view of pleasure to consume me. In Jesus' name. Amen.

Thought for Today

Day 11 - Perpetuate

Today's word is perpetuate, which is derived from perpetual. It means to continue or enduring forever or continue without interruption.

Our relationship with the Lord should be perpetual. We should remain in Christ perpetually as we endure the challenges of life, allowing our faith to increase and be stretched as described in Colossians 1:23a (TPT). It says "If indeed you continue to advance in faith, assured of a firm foundation to grow upon. Never be shaken from the hope of the gospel you have believed…"

To be perpetually in Christ creates a solid foundation for a lifetime. As we allow His word to mold our thoughts into His thoughts we will not be shaken by the issues of this world. We will go from glory to glory. Even when times are tough our faith will remain, and it will get us through when we are anchored in Him. There will be times when we will have to go after the Lord with all we have. Why? Because the enemy wants to pull us back into a dark world.

Do not allow the darkness of this world to interrupt your walk with the Lord. Be steadfast, unmovable, always abiding in HIM! Which reminds me of John 15:5 (NIV), "I am the vine; you are the branches. If you remain in me and I in you, you will bear much fruit; apart from me you can do nothing." We see from this scripture; it is imperative for us to abide in Christ so that we can do what He has called us to do and bear fruit or evidence of Him in our lives. Are you ready to be perpetual in your relationship with Christ?

Let's Pray:

Father, I come asking You to help me to remain perpetual in You. I pray my faith is not shaken but is steadfast and unmovable in You. I ask You, Lord, to help me bear Your fruit in everything I put my hands on. In Jesus' name. Amen.

Thought for Today

Day 12 - Proceed

Today's word is proceed, which means to move or go forward or onward; to continue one's course.

When we are on a spiritual journey with the Lord, the enemy will do everything possible to challenge our course. He will misdirect us or even get us to stop moving forward. We must keep our focus on the Lord, on the course He has provided or shown us.

It does not matter how good the world makes things look -don't take the bait. The things the Lord has for you will come to pass when you stay true to the call and the course you are on. The Lord loves you and wants to see you succeed in every area of your life. He sent His Holy Spirit to empower you to succeed.

The word of God tells us in 1 Corinthians 2:10-12 (NIV), "These are the things God has revealed to us by his Spirit. The Spirit searches all things, even the deep things of God. For who knows a person's thoughts except their own spirit within them? In the same way no one knows the thoughts of God except the Spirit of God. What we have received is not the spirit of the world, but the Spirit who is from God, so that we may understand what God has freely given us."

This makes us know that through the Spirit within us, we have the power to proceed in the direction the Lord has given us. Therefore, we must stay encouraged to keep going and not look back to the old life, situation, or habits.

Let's Pray:

Dear Lord, thank You for keeping me in You. I want to keep moving forward in You. I ask for Your guidance to the next level in my spiritual journey, that I may obtain the things You have for me and walk freely in them. In Jesus' name. Amen.

Thought for Today

Day 13 - Pursue

Today's word is pursue, which means to follow in order to overtake; chase; to strive to gain; seek to attain or accomplish; proceed in accordance with.

You want to continually pursue the plan of God for your life. Today, one must be diligent in pursuing the will of God because the world is in pursuit of you and wants to overtake you.

The definition of pursue is to strive to attain. The Bible tells us in Matthew 6:33 (NIV), "But seek first his kingdom and his righteousness, and all these things will be given to you as well."

So, when we pursue the will of God for our lives, which will include seeking Him. Pursue wisdom from Him, knowledge of Him, and pursue the understanding of His word from Him. Pursue His ways of doing life. This is hugely important if you want a continual, successful walk with the Lord.

The Bible is very clear about our pursuit of the Lord; Proverbs 16:3 (NKJV) says this, "Commit your works to the Lord, And your thoughts will be established." NIV says it this way, "Commit to the Lord whatever you do, and he will establish your plans." TPT says it this way, "Before you do anything, put your trust totally in God and not in yourself. Then every plan you make will succeed."

When we commit ourselves to the Lord or totally trust Him with our lives, our thoughts and plans are successfully established (brought about permanently). Who does not want to be successful?

Let's Pray:

Heavenly Father, I speak Matthew 6:33 over my life, that I will seek You and Your righteousness first each morning. In doing so, I will have Your mind and Your will over each task for the day. I pray that that You will add to me everything required to accomplish the tasks before me. I commit to You my day that You will guide me through it. In Jesus' name. Amen.

Thought for Today

Day 14 - Press

Today's word is press, which has many applicable definitions. For this devotion, we will focus on the following meanings of press: to act upon with steadily applied weight (push) or force; To move by weight (push) or force in a certain direction or certain position.

Have you ever been hard pressed to get to work, school or church on time? You may have pushed the limits of the law of the land by speeding down the street. Why? So, you could make it to your destination on time or within a reasonable time. How can we have that same zeal and drive to get to our God-given destination?

The apostle Paul teaches us in Philippians 3:14 (NLT), "I press on to reach the end of the race and receive the heavenly prize for which God, through Christ Jesus, is calling us."

So, in the same spirit that Paul has, we should press into the Holy Spirit and become relentless in reaching the place where God wants us to be. We may feel like we are alone at times, but remember, God said He will never leave you nor will He forsake you; He will be with you until the end of time.

There are a lot of things in this world that compete for our attention and time. however, we must press in and find our alone time with the Lord. Pray - Listen - Act! Hold on to the progress you have already made (Phil 3:16). Press on to the next level.

Let's Pray:

Father, I press in towards You, to receive my prize. I come against every distraction that attempts to stop me. I am determined to move in the direction You want me to go. Lord, I am ready to pray, listen and act upon the instructions You give me. In Jesus' name. Amen.

Thought for Today

Day 15 - Pain

Today's word is pain, meaning mental or emotional suffering or torment.

Let's be real, "pain" in the body of Christ is an actual manifestation for some. But we are not called to be tormented emotionally, mentally, or physically. There are many scriptures that speak about pain, but God is the source of our healing from any kind of pain.

Jeremiah 33:6 (NIV) says, "Nevertheless, I will bring health and healing to it; I will heal my people and will let them enjoy abundant peace and security."

You see, all the way back in the Old Testament, Jeremiah the prophet spoke of healing for God's people. Why? Because it is not the Father's will for us to be in pain sickness or torment.

When Jesus was nailed to the cross, He took upon himself all forms of sin, sicknesses, and diseases. 1 Peter 2:24 (NIV) says, "He himself bore our sins" in his body on the cross, so that we might die to sins and live for righteousness; "by his wounds you have been healed."

Again, the pain that is felt by individuals can be healed by the word of God. As we exercise our faith and believe the word of God, all things become possible and are possible through Christ. So, I encourage you to lean into the Lord. Put your trust totally in Him without leaning to your own understanding, but in all things acknowledge him as Lord, savior, and healer.

Let's Pray:

Heavenly Father, I thank You for Jesus Christ dying on the cross for my sins, sicknesses, and diseases. I choose today to believe the word of God for the pain I experience in my body. I decree that by the stripes of Jesus I am healed. Thank you, Lord. In Jesus' name. Amen.

Thought for Today

Day 16 - Pertinacious

The word of the day is pertinacious, which means holding tenaciously to a purpose, course of action.

Can you see yourself holding on to what God has called you to, put in your hand, or promised you? One thing I have discovered is that the enemy is in hot pursuit to stop us from living out the Lord's plan for our lives. Therefore, we must be pertinaciously seeking after the will of God for our lives.

We as believers have promises from the Lord, but we must push through to receive them. The apostle Paul reminds us in Ephesians 1:11 (KJV), "In whom also we have obtained an inheritance, being predestinated according to the purpose of him who worketh all things after the counsel of his own will..."

This is just one of many promises the Father has for his children. As we are abiding in Him, He will reveal to us other promises. He wants us to discover His purpose for our predestined lives through seeking and praying to Him. All we have to do is be pertinacious towards His purposes. For He is a God Who keeps His promises. Seek Him with your whole heart and he will be found. Just as we are pertinacious in our personal goals for our lives, we can be that way for the Lord.

Let's Pray:

Father God, I draw near to You asking for Your promises to me be made manifest in my life. Although I struggle to keep up with You and Your plans and purposes for me, I ask that You show me the way as I seek You with my whole heart. Bring me out of stagnation to be pertinaciously seeking after You. In Jesus' name. Amen.

Thought for Today

Day 17 - Pressure

Today's word is pressure, which means the exertion of force; a constraining or compelling force or influence; an urgency of affairs or business.

The world systems and ways put pressure on people in the form of influences to accept things that are in direct conflict with the word of God. It makes some people feel inadequate in their appearance, social status, and financial status. It makes people deny that Jesus is the son of God or that He was raised from the dead and is seated with the Heavenly Father.

The apostle Paul gives us a way to push back on the pressures of the world system. He teaches in Romans 12:1-2 (TPT), "Beloved friends, what should be our proper response to God's marvelous mercies? To surrender yourselves to God to be his sacred, living sacrifices. And live in holiness, experiencing all that delights his heart. For this becomes your genuine expression of worship. Stop imitating the ideals and opinions of the culture around you but be inwardly transformed by the Holy Spirit through a total reformation of how you think. This will empower you to discern God's will as you live a beautiful life, satisfying and perfect in his eyes."

You see, Paul provided the essence of how you and I can deal with the pressure of this world system. He advises us to push back the pressure with the word of God for any situation that threatens to tempt or destroy us. When we consistently renew our minds with the Word of Truth, the tendency to buy into the world system becomes null and void - especially when we measure everything against the Word of God.

Let's Pray:

Father I come before You today submitting myself to You. I do not deny the pressure of the world is great, but I do know greater is He who is in me than he that is in this world. Lord, I ask you to help me to hold fast to the Word of God to fight against the pressure of the systems of this world and follow after You. In Jesus' name. Amen.

Thought for Today

Day 18 - Preserve

Today's word is preserve, which means to keep alive or in existence; to turn from harm, protect, spare.

Have you ever experienced a potentially life-threatening event, only to have your life preserved or spared? In spite of the threat, you continue to live and exist! In this instance, John 10:10 is in effect, saying, "the thief (devil) comes only to steal and kill and destroy." Overall, that is what the enemy wants to do, and he will use any means to do it.

However, the Lord has a different plan for you and I. Jesus said, in the second half of John 10:10 (NIV), "I have come that they (you) may have life, and have it to the full (fullness)." Now He is the best preserver of life one can ever expect to have!

Jesus offers us life and gives us an opportunity to accept it. He, Jesus, is the way the truth and the life (John. 14:6). As we walk with Him, He will preserve our lives. Yes, the enemy will come at you, but remember, he has been defeated. We are overcomers!

Psalm 138:7 (NIV) says, "Though I walk in the midst of trouble, you preserve my life. You stretch out your hand against the anger of my foes; with your right hand you save me." Wow, it is so good to know that the Lord preserves our lives. In the middle of our storms, He is there to save us.

Will you allow the loving Father God, through Jesus Christ, to preserve your life? He will keep you from all harm. He will protect you from the terror at night. He will preserve you for the work He has for you on this earth. He will show you and direct you to His perfect will for your life.

Let's Pray:

Father thank you for preserving my life. I am ready to walk in Your will. I ask You to lead me in the direction I should go and preserve me along the way from the attacks of the enemy. In Jesus' name. Amen.

Thought for Today

Day 19 - Protection

Today's word is protection, which means being protected or preservation from injury or harm.

God is our ultimate protector. Even when we cannot see him in a situation, He is there. There are many times we may feel, "I got this." We take Gods' protection for granted, walking through life as if we have no cares in the world and nothing will happen to us that we cannot handle.

However, if the truth be told, we are walking under the protection of grace and mercy, and under the prayer covering of our parents, grandparents, and others. The Lord wants us to be aware of the constant protection He provides for us.

The Bible tells us in Psalms 91:1-2 (NIV), "Whoever dwells in the shelter of the Most High will rest in the shadow of the Almighty. I will say of the LORD, "He is my refuge and my fortress, my God, in whom I trust."

The Lord wants us to dwell in His presence for our protection. He wants us to lean in on Him of our own free will and not depend on others for prayer or safety. In Psalms 91:9-10 (TPT) it says, "When we live our lives within the shadow of God Most High, our secret hiding place, we will always be shielded from harm. How then could evil prevail against us or disease infect us?"

God is the ultimate protector! I am reminded of Isaiah 54:17 (NKJV), "No weapon formed against you shall prosper, And every tongue which rises against you in judgment You shall condemn. This is the heritage of the servants of the Lord..."

Let's Pray:

Father God, thank you so much for Your protection! I make You my hiding place when the enemy comes; I know that You, Almighty, will protect me. I stand on Your promises and the heritage given to me knowing no weapon formed against me will prosper. In Jesus' name. Amen!

Thought for Today

Day 20 - Process

Today's word is process, meaning to have a systematic series of actions directed to some end.

I have heard and even said on occasion, "Trust the process." Although this slogan is best known in the sports arena and its culture, it basically means, although things are looking bad right now, there is a plan in place that will make it better.

Personally, when I use the term, I am referring to the Lord's way of making things better, in spite of what one sees. The word of God declares this in Jeremiah 29:11 (NIV), "For I know the plans I have for you, declares the Lord, plans to prosper you and not to harm you, plans to give you hope and a future."

Most times, when life throws us a curveball, it catches us off guard and we have no insight on getting through the situation. However, as believers, we must understand - the Lord God, already has a plan to bring us through. The process is pictured in Jeremiah 29:12-14 (NIV), which says, "Then you will call on me and come and pray to me, and I will listen to you. You will seek me and find me when you seek me with all your heart. I will be found by you, declares the Lord, and will bring you back from captivity. I will gather you from all the nations and places where I have banished you," declares the Lord, "and will bring you back to the place from which I carried you in exile."

We also find a process in Matthew 6:33, "But seek first his kingdom and his righteousness, and all these things will be given to you as well." and Matthew 7:7-8, "Ask and it will be given to you; seek and you will find; knock and the door will be opened to you. For everyone who asks receives; the one who seeks finds; and to the one who knocks, the door will be opened." God's process always contains actionable steps to get us where He wants us to be.

Let's Pray:

Father, I trust your process for my life. Your ways are better than any ways I can ever imagine. I will trust You even when I can't see you moving because I know You are moving on my behalf. So, Lord, move mightily in my life, In Jesus' name. Amen.

Thought for Today

Day 21 - Praise

Today's word is praise, which means the act of expressing admiration, offering of grateful homage in words or song, an act of worship.

Wow, so much can be said about praise. We could easily narrow it down to the grateful homage in words or in song; but in reality, praise is a lifestyle.

Living a life of praise is easier than one may think. That is, when you are doing it through the empowering of the Holy Spirit and the presence of the Lord. Hebrews 13:15 (NIV) says, "Through Jesus, therefore, let us continually offer to God a sacrifice of praise—the fruit of lips that openly profess his name."

In the scripture, "continually" means all the time in good and troubled times, we are to give a sacrificial praise. To be continually in praise...that is truly a lifestyle.

We see in Psalms 63:3-4 (NIV) it tells us, "Because your love is better than life, my lips will glorify you. I will praise you as long as I live, and in your name, I will lift up my hands."

> Praise is a way of life.
> Praise is what I do.
> I will praise you in the morning.
> I will praise you in the noon.
> I will praise you in the evening.

Psalm 150:6 (NIV) says this, "Let everything that has breath praise the Lord. Praise the Lord." We are part of that "everything,, so let us praise Him, The Lord God Almighty!

Let's Pray:

Father I praise You; I lift You up; I give You all the Glory! When I open my mouth in the morning, I will praise you, before I lay my head to sleep, I will praise You! May every part of my being praise You Lord God! In Jesus' name. Amen!

Thought for Today

Day 22 - Patience

Today's word is patience, which means an ability or willingness to suppress restlessness or annoyance when confronted with delay. It is the quality of being patient.

Most people are afraid to pray for patience. This is because of the notion that praying for patience will bring on afflictions; and no one wants to deal with afflictions. But let me tell you, that is not the case with our loving Father. He does not use afflictions to teach lessons or to bring on patience.

From our definition, we understand patience as having the ability to suppress restlessness. To tie the word of God back to this understanding; let's look at Psalm 27:14 (NIV), "Wait for the Lord; be strong and take heart and wait for the Lord." You see, waiting on the Lord helps us develop patience. When we are in our quiet time we should pray to the Lord, then wait on Him to speak to us. Slow the mind down by meditating on the word of God. As it is said in our scripture, "Be strong and take heart." Waiting creates a strong heart that embodies patience.

Everything we experience in life is used in some way to produce patience. We learned in James 1:2-4 (AMP), "Consider it nothing but joy, my brothers and sisters, whenever you fall into various trials. Be assured that the testing of your faith [through experience] produces endurance [leading to spiritual maturity, and inner peace]. And let endurance have its perfect result and do a thorough work, so that you may be perfect and completely developed [in your faith], lacking in nothing."

Verse three talks about the testing of our faith; it is through life experiences that we develop inner peace, which is in essence, 'patience.' When we walk out verse four, we are to 'LET' or allow endurance to have perfect results, doing a thorough work in us. As a result, we will become perfect and completely developed in our faith.

Let's Pray:

Father, I thank You for the work of patience You are doing in my life. I will "let" the process of endurance work in my life, producing the fruit of patience. In doing so, I will walk in joy through every trial knowing You are in control. In Jesus' name. Amen.

Thought for Today

Day 23 - Peace

Today's word is peace, which means a state of mutual harmony between people or groups, freedom from any strife or dissension.

In today's society, peace is a constant prayer for many people across the United States and throughout the world. There is much turmoil in each of our countries, states, cities, and neighborhoods. We want peace!

As individuals, we can have peace amid the world chaos. However, as we meditate on Isaiah 26:3 (NIV), which says, "You will keep in perfect peace those whose minds are steadfast, because they trust in you." When we become intentional about spending time with God, not only do we develop peace of mind, but our faith and trust in Him increase. The peace of God allows us to walk in peace when issues arise in the workplace or any other areas of life because we keep our mind steadfastly focused on Him.

Romans 12:18 (NIV) tells us, "If it is possible, as far as it depends on you, live at peace with everyone." The message Paul is conveying here is that at some point in our walk, we will cross paths with something or someone that will try to disrupt our peace. He said, "as far as it depends on you," meaning you have a choice as to how you choose to respond; you can take the high road and keep the peace, or you can take the low road and go face-to-face with them. We get to choose if we will walk in peace.

Let's Pray:

Father, I thank You for the peace that surpasses all understanding. I choose this day to walk in peace. I choose this day to keep my mind steadfastly on You; for You are the peacemaker. In all the chaos of today, I choose You; I choose peace. In Jesus' name. Amen.

Thought for Today

Day 24 - Possibility

Today's word is possibility, which means something possible. Possible means that it may or can be, exist, happen, be done, be used, etc.

Do you have an assignment (spiritual or natural) that looks like an impossible task? You may have looked at it from several angles with an attempt to figure out how to even get started, but to no avail, it sits there undone looking back at you!

Let me encourage you to take that task and lay it at the feet of Jesus. In Matthew 19:26 (NIV), Jesus tells us "...With man (woman) this is impossible, but with God all things are possible." You see, the assignment or task that we struggle with becomes clear when we put it before the Lord. He will show us how to tackle it. He will give us the exact steps to carry it out and it will work out.

How do we know this will work? Good question. James tells us in James 1:6 (NIV) "But when you ask, you must believe and not doubt, because the one who doubts is like a wave of the sea, blown and tossed by the wind."

The key here is...you have to ask the Lord; then you must believe He will do what you ask. Even when you cannot see it immediately, you resolve in your spirit that He is doing it on your behalf. So, keep in mind, with the Lord all things are possible. Every task or assignment He gives you is made possible when you present it to the Lord for guidance and directions.

Let's Pray:

Father, I am so grateful that You can make this impossible task possible. I lay it at Your feet asking You to lead and guide me on how to get it done. Lord, I wait on You and believe You at Your word that all things are possible to those who believe and not doubt. Thank You for Your guidance. In Jesus' name. Amen.

Thought for Today

Day 25 - Passion

Today's word is passion, which means any powerful or compelling emotion or feeling; the state of being acted upon or affected by something external.

What are you passionate about? What moves you to action? When you can answer these questions, you have identified the thing you are passionate about. This "thing" brings about an overwhelming compelling feeling that drives you. You become passionate about it.

When we think of Jesus' compassion for us and how it drove Him to give His life, that is a compassionate display of love. As we read Colossians chapter 3, keep in mind all the Lord has already done for you and I as He made us alive in Him. In Colossians 3:12 (NIV) it says, "Therefore, as God's chosen people, holy and dearly loved, clothe yourselves with compassion, kindness, humility, gentleness, and patience."

As we walk out the thing the Lord has given us a strong compassion for; our interaction with others should bear this verse as we wear these descriptions in our hearts: we are clothed with compassion! Our compassion for the Lord should keep us humble before Him, strengthened in Him and empowered by Him to do what He says we can do.

In addition, since we wear compassion, kindness, humility, gentleness, and patience our response to others will be from that posture. Even when others cannot understand the assignment we are compassionate about, we still walk it out in this posture.

Let's Pray:

Dear Lord, as I sit at Your feet, I worship You. I thank You for all You have done in and through my life. Thank You for clothing me with compassion, kindness, humility, gentleness, and patience. My passion for _____, consumes me and I lay it at Your feet so You may show me how to walk it out. I ask You to order my steps and direct my path so that I may be pleasing to You with what You have entrusted to me. In Jesus' name. Amen.

Thought for Today

Day 26 - Pride

Today's word is pride, meaning a high or inordinate opinion of one's own dignity, importance, merit, or superiority whether as cherished in the mind or as a display in bearing, conduct, etc.

Pride is a place where we do not want to find ourselves. God warns us about pride throughout the Bible. In Romans 12:16 (TPT), Paul teaches us, "Live happily together in a spirit of harmony, and be as mindful of another's worth as you are your own. Don't live with a lofty mind-set, thinking you are too important to serve others, but being willing to do menial tasks and identify with those who are humble minded. Don't be smug or even think for a moment that you know it all."

We are not better than those who we walk with daily. Each of us must answer to the Lord as to how we are interacting with others. If we find ourselves walking in pride, the Lord will have us to deal with it. As the word of God says in Isaiah 2:11 (NLT), "Human pride will be brought down, and human arrogance will be humbled. Only the Lord will be exalted on that day of judgment."

I don't know about you, but I would rather give up pride myself than for the Lord to humble me! Finally, keep in mind that Lucifer failed because he allowed pride to exalt him; in his mind, he was above God. Let us not exalt ourselves higher than others.

Let's Pray:

Father God, I humble myself before You. Lord, I do not want to exalt myself above anyone. I ask You to create in me a pure heart. Look at my heart, and if there is anything there that is not pleasing to You, I ask You to remove it. In Jesus' name. Amen.

Thought for Today

Day 27 - Pant

Today's word is pant, which means to long with breathless or intense eagerness, to yearn.

Have you ever desired something so badly that you literally panted after it with strong intense eagerness? We see in Psalms 42:1-2 (NIV), "As a deer pants for streams of water, so my soul pants for you, my God. My soul thirsts for God, for the living God. When can I go and meet with God?"

We long for God, we long for Him like a deer pants for water - we do not stop searching. Daily, we come to the brook to drink of the living water. When our souls pants for God, we have become serious about our relationship with Him. You can meet God anytime you desire early in the morning, at midday, in the evening or in the midnight hour. He's waiting to meet you in that secret place to commune with you.

Psalm 119: 131 (TPT) goes on to say, "I open my mouth and inhale the Word of God because I crave the revelation of your commands." Are we ready to open our mouths and pant or inhale God's words, His revelation, and commands from the Lord our God? We should get to that place. Are we willing to allow space for him in our lives at a new level?

God is waiting for us to come into the chambers and meet with Him so He can unfold His word to us, bringing us light and understanding. Will you meet Him there?

Let's Pray:

Father God, I desire, I pant for, and I crave Your words, Your revelation, and commands! I open my mouth and inhale every Word You speak to me. I long to be near You, in Your presence! Speak to me Lord, I will obey, I will receive, I do believe, and I will walk out Your Word daily. In Jesus' name. Amen.

Thought for Today

Day 28 - People

Today's word is people, which speaks for itself, as persons, men, women, or children.

We cannot live this life without the involvement of people. No matter what school, career, or service you find yourself in; you will be around people.

I recently heard a pastor say ministry would be easier if we did not have people in it. That was a funny statement; but the reality is, there are people everywhere we turn. This world is made up of people – people of many diverse types, shapes, etc. That was part of God's plan when He created man according to his likeness. When His image bearers chose incorrectly in Genesis chapter one, God knew He had to make a way for mankind to continue to commune with Him.

Therefore, in John chapter 3, Father God unveiled His plan for people to continue to commune with Him. In John 3:5 (NIV), it says, "Jesus answered, '"Very truly I tell you, no one can enter the kingdom of God unless they are born of water and the Spirit.'"

God's plan in John 3:16 (NIV) says, "For God so loved the world (people) that he gave his one and only Son, that whoever believes in him shall not perish but have eternal life." So, since God loves people, and we want the will of God for our lives, then we too, must learn to love people. It is with people that ministry calls come about. People make up families. It is with families that churches are filled. People need the Lord.

Let's Pray:

Lord, thank you for people, because I am one of many people. I need You, Lord! I pray You will show me the individuals You will have me to speak to, minister to, or pray for, and that You will use me to reveal Yourself to them. I Pray as a whole for people whose paths I cross. Let me show them Your love and Your light. In Jesus' name. Amen.

Thought for Today

Day 29 - Promote

Today's word is promote, which means to help or encourage to exist, flourish or further. It is to advance in rank or position.

Many times, when we hear the word promotion, we automatically associate it with our jobs or place of work. However, there are other ways of seeing promotion in our lives. Today, we will look at the definition differently; we will focus on it as to encourage to exist, flourish, or further our walk with Jesus.

Let's start by considering a lifestyle change. Proverbs 16:3 (NIV) tells us, "Commit to the Lord whatever you do, and he will establish your plans." Established here means to make successful. When we commit our plans to God and trust Him with the outcome, we set ourselves up for success, because He promotes or further those plans along. He causes them to flourish. Therefore, that lifestyle change will be successful as the Lord establishes it in our hearts.

First Peter 5:6 (NIV) says, "Humble yourselves, therefore, under God's mighty hand, that he may lift you up in due time."

If we humble ourselves before God in admission that we need Him, then He will exalt us to a place of honor and promote that lifestyle change as we put it before Him.

You see, promotion comes in many forms other than our place of work. God wants us to be successful in every area of our lives. He is waiting to promote our efforts to a place of honor before Him. We simply must trust Him without leaning on our own knowledge of how to change our lifestyles. We must trust the Lord with whatever it is that we present before Him.

Let's Pray:

Father I thank You that promotion comes from You. I commit myself to You. I commit to You all my ideas and plans, asking that You will establish them according to Your will. I will put aside anything that is not in Your will and will patiently wait for plans to come to pass when that is what You require of me. As I humble myself before you, I await your timing for promotion. In Jesus' name. Amen.

Thought for Today

Day 30 - Plans

Today's word is plans, which means a scheme or method of acting, doing, preceding, making, etc. It is to draw or make a diagram or layout of an object or thing.

There is a cliche that says, "to fail to plan is to plan to fail." Going through life with no plans is a sure set up for failure. Yes, I believe the Lord orders the steps of the righteous person. God impresses a direction in our lives. Our job is to follow His direction.

In order for us to remember God's directions, we write them down in a planner or write the vision, as in Habakkuk 2:2. Then we can assuredly stand on the promise of God as noted in Jeremiah 29:11 (NIV); "For I know the plans I have for you, declares the Lord, plans to prosper you and not to harm you, plans to give you a hope and a future."

God has great plans for our lives. The next big win will come for us when we directly line up with His will for our lives. The word of God says in Philippians 2:13 (NIV) "For it is God who works in you to will and to act in order to fulfill his good purpose." God willed for us to walk in His purpose. We sometimes act upon His will thinking it is our own great idea, but God is continually working in and through us to fulfill His purpose on earth.

So, where do we go from here? Go to God in prayer; ask for His will and purpose for your life. Pray He will work his plan into your life. Be humble before Him; be obedient to Him; and keep submitting your plans to Him so you may be established.

Let's Pray:

Father, thank You for the plans and purposes You have already birthed in me. I lay them before You for directions. I pray Your will be done in my life as I am humble before You. Lord, I pray for Your will to be made plain to me and that I understand it. Thank You, Lord, for leading and guiding me. In Jesus' name. Amen.

Thought for Today

Day 31 - Promise

Today's word is promise, which means a declaration that something will or will not be done, given etc. It is an expression of assurance of an expectation.

As the definition states, we should always declare God's promises over our lives. In doing so, it strengthens our assurance of the word of God for each of us individually. Here are a few of God's promises for our lives.

God has a plan for your life:

Jeremiah 29:11 (NIV) says, "For I know the plans I have for you," declares the Lord, "plans to prosper you and not to harm you, plans to give you hope and a future."

God promised to strengthen and help us:

Isaiah 41:10 (NIV) says, "So do not fear, for I am with you; do not be dismayed, for I am your God. I will strengthen you and help you; I will uphold you with my righteous right hand."

God promised to give us the desires of our heart:

Psalm 37:4 (NIV) "Take delight in the LORD, and he will give you the desires of your heart."

God promised that those who look for Him will find Him:

Jeremiah 29:13 (NIV) "You will seek me and find me when you seek me with all your heart."

God promises to give us what we ask for:

John 15:7 (NIV) "If you remain in me and my words remain in you, ask whatever you wish, and it will be done for you."

The Lord promises to work out our issues:

Romans 8:28 (NIV) "And we know that in all things God works for the good of those who love him, who have been called according to his purpose."

The Lord promises to complete His work in us:

Philippians 1:6 (NIV) "Being confident of this, that he who began a good work in you will carry it on to completion until the day of Christ Jesus."

The Lord promises to meet our needs:

Philippians 4:19 (NIV) "And my God will meet all your needs according to the riches of his glory in Christ Jesus."

The Lord promises if we seek Him, He will add to us:

Matthew 6:33 (NIV) "But seek first his kingdom and his righteousness, and all these things will be given to you as well."

So, as we spend time reminding ourselves of God's promises, we can remind God of His promises to us as we pray them back to Him. He delights in our fellowship with Him.

Let's Pray:

Father, I thank you for Your promises as they are yes and amen. You are a good, good Father! I stand on Your promises and ask that Your will be done. I am strengthened each time I am reminded of a promise You have made to me. Thank you, Lord, for fulfilling Your promises to me. In Jesus' name. Amen.

Thought for Today

About the Author

Frizella Taylor is a wife, mother, grandmother, ordained minister, author, conference speaker, writing coach and entrepreneur.

Frizella's writing career began over 20 years ago. She has written and published eight books to date. She has composed and written several types of books. Her Christian background has provided her with a wealth of leadership experiences (i.e., children's ministry, youth ministry, women ministry, prayer, and intercessory ministry as well as Pastoral) to glean from and share. You may find her books at www.TaylorMadePublishingFL.com/frizella-taylor.

Frizella's formal education includes a master's degree in Information Technology, Bachelor of Science in Management and Business, and an associate degree in Computer Programming.

Frizella and her husband, Steve, own TaylorMade Publishing LLC of Florida, providing services to authors in the areas of coaching, proofreading, editing, formatting, eBooks, book publishing, book promotion videos, and author websites.

You can learn more about TaylorMade Publishing LLC at www.TaylorMadePublishingFL.com.